the tearing sound

www.amplifypublishinggroup.com

The Tearing Sound

©2022 Ron Berube. All Rights Reserved. No part of this publication may be reproduced, stored in a retrieval system or transmitted in any form by any means electronic, mechanical, or photocopying, recording or otherwise without the permission of the author.

For more information, please contact:
Mascot Books, an imprint of Amplify Publishing Group
620 Herndon Parkway, Suite 320
Herndon, VA 20170
info@amplifypublishing.com

Library of Congress Control Number: 2022903921

CPSIA Code: PRV0722A

ISBN-13: 978-1-64543-844-1

Printed in the United States

the tearing sound

CONTENTS

For Christie

You'd like a poem
about how much I love you.
That's not how it works.
     Each word alters what I write,
     as your love does who I am.

———

A Warning

We live among you
and when you least expect it
we're writing poems.

———

African Lines

after Motherwell, "Africa Suite #7"

Once upon a time a long time ago
a man who did not know he was a man
drew a picture of a deer in the dirt.
Another man who did not know he was a man
looked at the picture and pointed the way
and the two men stood up together and left.
The deer they found was already dead
and jackals had eaten its flesh.
The two men who did not know they were men
broke open the bones of the deer with a stone
and ate the marrow that was in them.
They followed the jackals and found them
eating a body that looked like their own
and one of them touched its eyes.
In that moment he knew that he was alive
and he understood that he was a man
and he looked at the other man
and he knew that he knew too.
He drew a line in the dirt with his hand
and next to the line he drew another line
that bent back to where it began.
The two men who knew they were men
looked at that sign and they understood
that it meant that they knew they were men,
and when others saw it they knew not
what it meant unless they knew they were men.
And in this way they knew each other
once upon a time a long time ago.

———

Adam and Eve

Which one saw the other first,
Sapiens or Neandertal?
And was it fear or fascination
that held their gaze? Us or them
was always the primal calculation,
the one we're still buggered by
today. Let's not romanticize
what happened. They both
no doubt were hairy brutes
and estrus I imagine was
the source of that attraction,
their coupling likely something
we see daily with our dogs,
involving just as much
of love. But maybe, just maybe,
the one with those heavy brows
gave a pierced and ochre-stained
piece of shell to the one
who looked different, more gracile,
and tall. Perhaps she smiled.

———

The Oil of Us

Worse comes to worst
we'll be huddled where it's
warm in winter cool in summer
in a cave overlooking the sea
or the desert plains wondering
who else has survived and leave
for those who will later use
the oil of us to comfort
their still living bones ochre-stained
prints of our hands on the walls
as we've done from the first
if only to say we were here.

———

Chauvet

Drawn out in cave light,
horses whinny on the walls,
running still to us.

———

Astronomy

Meteor shower.
We're all spinning here below,
hominins in thrall

———

How Far to the Horizon

At certain times the sea and sky assume
a curious shade of cloudy blue and cause
their commissure to disappear and sailing ships
to float in air where many things are deemed
to be that otherwise would not while you remain
ashore to wonder just how far, how long,
or is it Zeno's god damn paradox again,
the name on the tip of the tongue, the word
to which neurons send no more an axon,
where the ends of the bridge don't meet
in the middle but the middle joins the ends
and koans bob in the waves like buoys
to mark your way and people cry when you
at last arrive because they know you're going
to leave and cheer when you leave knowing
you'll return, where everything you hope for
is what you nonetheless cannot believe.

———

The Tearing Sound

Like pulling teeth, the way my father tied
a string from my incisor
to a knob, said, Just relax, and slammed the door,
his grandfather wrapped a rope
around the stump and slapped a horse's rump
as plant and muscle fibers
strained and roots began to tear and soon
a hole filled up with blood.

Dirt but reluctantly submits to deeds
and bides its time before
it pushes old rocks up and children off,
for whom the tearing sound
will out like blood when they try haltingly
to explain themselves, say why
they have to leave and promise they'll return,
among the loved ones weeping.

We've always followed rivers to their end,
like teleologies,
little or no thought given to the source,
just a little trickle
from some unseen once glacial mountaintop,
surprisingly pristine,
where nature broke solid rocks apart,
let ancient water forth.

We stand on old bones everywhere.
Regret hides itself below
but we have marked the spots with stones,
return and visit them
like toddlers to grandparents who embrace
and say they understand
when young tongues dig around new teeth, unearth
no words, only feelings.

Excavate the ground beneath your feet,
you may end up standing in mid-air,
wondering what's that sound you hear.

———

Full Moon

The few clouds straggling behind
the departing front have finally left
the wet sand damascene in the light
of the moon's full unshadowed face
circled by a numinous haze,
the scars of ancient impacts
human to our hopeful minds
after a day of rain, of shadows and winds
with a clarity so eloquently still
even the dogs that by habit bay at
and about it sit stunned into silence.
This is what our shorter, longer-limbed, hairier
forebears saw making them think
there is something there,
there is something more.

—————

Something

for James and Geoffrey

It was of course a shock
though we weren't really close.
He'd call at night to talk
when he drank and got morose.

More often lately now I can't
remember quite how things will end.
Is it just a game of chance?
There's so much that depends.

So what is it this time?
We all live in the past,
and try to make it rhyme,
as if it then might last.

There's always something though.
That's the beauty of it.

———————

Beachcombing

Walking the edge of the ocean,
my memory-impaired mother and I,
our eyes straining the surf for a conch
not yet broken though tossed and scarred,
she takes my arm and stops,
says, Sir, how large
must a small shard be
to still evoke the shell?

————

Don in His Chair

Don sits in the mouth of his garage
in a weathered rocking chair with
a lifetime's worth of yard sale
bargains and mechanic's tools
stacked and crammed against
the walls, looks down the length
of his driveway at as much
of the world pass by as he can see
from there. He sees pretty well
straight ahead but says anymore
he can't hear shit, and when we
hail each other as we often do I'll
sometimes holler something like,
"Gonna be another hot one!" and he'll
holler something back like,
"She's visiting her sister!" Yesterday
he waved me over, said, "I saw you
talking to my Dad. Can you tell me
what he said?" I looked in his cloudy
eyes for help as he looked for it
in mine and shouted in his ear, "He
said everything's gonna be okay."
Don nodded grimly, said,
"I understand," patted me
on the shoulder and limped
into his house, where he always sits
on a couch from which he can
rarely get up by himself but
where it's cooler, under the fan.

———

Winter Window

Warm day in winter.
Old man opens a window.
Memories swarm in.

———

Winter Thief

Cold, low-lying sun
slips the slats of my window,
steals my winter sleep.

———

Herbal Sense

Basil grew beneath the bedroom window
in those days when we were both
but twenty-something, borrowing
each other's body every night, often
during the day as well, whenever
our hormones were not busy
otherwise. A summer breeze
was all it took to ruffle
the herbal leaves outside, waft
aromatic molecules through the screen.
Sometimes the oil-anointed fragrance
came at just the right coital moment
to make it seem we'd begotten it
with the intensity of our fucking. Thus
memories on occasion may be made.
Those plants of course grew stiff and dry
in time but if we cut store-bought basil
in the kitchen now idle hormones still
might be aroused to service,
dinner be delayed.

———————

Suburbia, Saturday Morning, Early

Weed whackers already whining.
Sirens, the shifting gears
of the trash pick-up trucks,
but abruptly, a moment enough
of silence that I can hear birds
chirping, and you beside me say,
Let's fuck. Soon, the sighing.
And always of course the prolonged,
discordant continuo of the dogs.

————

Canine Dreams

I'd wanted just to wander off
and lie with my old dog
who used to kick my kidneys
as he dreamt he chased
tongue lolling sideways
feral scents and I got stiff again
behind your legs when you had come
so quickly back no more wanting to
than I remain alone thank god
one of us always seems to know
that love is bred in blood and bone
and often must when needed
most be run to ground.

———

Nest, Egg

The bird chose poorly the place
for its nest too close
despite so thickly leaved
and twigged to a path
that children took to school
winding as it did through
woods untrammeled otherwise
who thought of it nothing
when their flailing arms
and careless cries put her
to flight in fear or for
distraction but creating
only an attraction found
then all-too early
the tightly-woven clutch
and removed with intently
gentle care the fragile
vessel of gestation
with a sense of wonder
too complex for them
to untangle or more naturally
to express than by saying simply,
"god."

———————

Rabbit Ears

The DNA for rabbits must say, First,
make ears. That's how I knew
they weren't moles when I exposed
the nest while mowing creeper
that was taking over, propagating like,
well, like rabbits do. Only two,
in a shallow bowl no bigger
than a cupping of your hand, curled
over each other, likely blind as yet
but with already outsized ears that said,
Stay clear, bunnies here;
we'll soon be living but
misleading metaphors for cute and cuddly.
For they don't always take to being held.
I've had my arm well-raked
by a bunny's claws to learn that lesson.
We create the metaphors, of course,
that survive only as they mean anything to us.
When Eostre, erstwhile goddess of the Spring,
discovered a bird with frozen wings,
she gave it new life as a rabbit,
so fast on its lucky feet it seemed to fly,
and more miraculously still was able to lay eggs,
themselves ancient symbols of fertility
the Anglo-Saxons fancifully painted
and gave away as gifts to celebrate the season.

Their credulity continues to amuse
if not amaze us, and their customs
seemed quaint to earnest Christians too,
who convinced them, one way or another,
to believe instead in a god who had risen
at Easter from the dead. Why
is there a plus sign on that building's roof?
my grade school daughter asked
as we drove past a church, and What
are those funny wires on Grandpa's old tee-vee?
as I excavated the remote
from the ageless cushions of the couch.
I covered up the nest with leaves and brush
and left the bunnies to their mother's care,
if not to that of fate and Mother Nature,
having also turned up with my mower lately
the surprisingly silky and delicate
discarded skin of a snake.

———

Beekeeping

It was a bee
the size of a songbird,
sounded like a flying
lawnmower, terrified
the dog. We used to put out
pots of flowers for them
in the summer but then
it was summer all the time
and we were hacking flora
with our butcher knives
just to open doors,
worried less about
an apiarian allergy
than a stinger that can
pierce your heart. The knives
make handy weapons too
against the bees but
as with their tiny
progenitors it's best
just to leave them be.
They're out for nectar not
your blood but don't
make a flower of yourself
with brightly colored clothes,
if you're still wearing those.
We're having to learn a new
relationship to nature, as if
we were not part of it
ourselves. It was a bee,
dancing, trying
to tell us something.

Eco Haiku

The moon holds its breath
The tide hesitates
As Neptune writhes in our net

______

Climate Change

Were we there today
would we sneer at the rumblings
in ancient Pompeii?

______

Letter to Gracchus

Can I be living in Pompeii listening
to people say that an eruption won't come soon
at every party I attend these days? Are not
these rumblings being felt and measurements made
by the hour, are things not getting worse, do you believe
in such reports? Have you seen by the way the new
fresco at Tullio's? I know, a weak reprise
of Apelles. It shows a satyr planted in
a maenad that I swear is Prilla. Don't I know
those eyes, that tattoo of clematis tendrils
climbing up her thigh? Old story, eh? But
am I lucky to be rid of her, will she still eat
a man alive? I miss her, Gracchus. Will you dine
with me in Paestum? I'm to meet a man about
a boat there and I would buy one of those conch shells
that one can find at all the little seaside shacks.

———————

Letter to Prilla

As I write I'm looking, Prilla, at the curling
tendril of smoke that's rising from Vesuvius.
It reminds me of the tattoo of clematis
climbing from your ankle up your thigh and how I
used to trace it with my tongue. I thought when I saw
your image on the wall at Tullio's that you
knew someday I would, and that your smirk was meant
for me. Or am I a bee that thinks a pollen grain
was put there just for him? You were always so, Come
hither, no go away, and I have never learned
the lesson. Is that why you ran, all part of your plan?
Don't tell me you didn't know I'd be at Gracchus'
house last night. We were counting on it, he and I.
He sat me on a banquette in the back, with
two Scythian girls, one of whom had taken my
balls in hand when you paraded queenly into
the room. My heart began to pound and my cock got
hard, solely because of you. Poor girl'd been working
a broken-handled pump til you showed up and up
I jumped. Even the ground was trembling, although that
was likely just Vesuvius, trying again to be portentous.
We're just playthings of the gods, you know,
even when we're striving hardest not to be. Should
we defy them, they'd say, Just as we'd foreseen.
Let's pretend that we do what we will, despite
what may be true. What else can we do? Let's pretend
we've never met, and find each other again. Let's
pretend that we're in love, if only for one night.
You can run off later, while I pretend to sleep.

———

Letter to Lucullus

for Jim & Alanna, who won't leave

I've loaded a cart to leave, Lucullus, at last.
Today's quake cracked my cistern, and as you
once said, a wise Roman needs no haruspex
for reading auguries. I've not yet recovered
from the last eruption, fifteen or so years ago.
It's hard to know what to take, although
I'm sure what you'll choose first and carefully
wrap in straw's that plaster Priapus
from your foyer with the outsized cock.
At least you'll always have something
to strive for. But I have an impediment
that's heavier than that. Its name -
stay with me now - is Prilla. I hear you
howl, but I'm in love, and we are resolved
to stay together. You may announce it –
as I know you will, and wouldn't have you
feel disloyal - at the baths tomorrow
in Sorrentum, should you make it. Tell it right,
it might earn you a dinner invite. Just be sure
to make it lurid. Insatiate lust, that's the thing.
You must make me a legend, friend. I depend
on you, for I may not be able to account
for myself. Prilla feels yet no need to flee.
I don't agree but I could no more leave her
than my legs. What am I to do? Sacrifice
my last ox? Our fate is what it is and trying
to escape it is just running faster in the rain.
What we would control is staying together.

Should the house fall upon us, here we still
will be. I know an old Oscan man whose
family survived the wars of Sulla, who can
remember when this was not a Roman town.
I often imagine prior peoples walking on
these same stones. If someday Pompeii has gone
the way of ancient Troy and the landscape
here is lousy with Roman ruins, perhaps
our bones will remain intact, with my legs
still between the two of hers. Vale, Lucullus.
That's my choice. You will when and if
you get this have made yours.

————

Marsyas on the Dock

Marsyas took the bait,
a lyre left by Apollo on a whim
to lure some hapless human to his fate.
Marsyas taught himself to play it,
then had the balls to challenge
the oracle's god to a musical duel.
He lost, of course. Apollo
outshined him on the scales.
To punish him for his hubris,
Apollo had Marsyas flayed alive,
which seems to us at best unjust.
It was a scene that many artists
over time have painted: Marsyas restrained
and being much too closely shaved;
sure to make the artist's name.
Sensational always sells, a timeless hook,
but what were they trying to tell themselves,
the Greeks, besides not to overreach?
Though there seems in it today
but little wisdom, even Homer knew
one job of any artist is to keep
the audience in their seats.

The rubber-aproned fisherman, with the butt
of a cold cigar pinched between his teeth,
makes one skilled slit at the gills, then peels
the skin back quickly to the tail with a
                RRRRRRRIP
so sudden and loud it shocks us,
and with a practiced flip he tosses
the skin to the crabs beneath
the slippery deck. With another swipe
of his long thin knife a pale fillet
slides boneless into a bucket. He does it
again, and again, and again –
fish after fish after fish –
the slit, the rip, the flip, the swipe –
and we are all transfixed,
until we're pulled by our bored children
impatiently back to the boats.

————

The Bones

for Frank

woke up cold and stumbled
pushing feet into pants went
into stubbled fields where clouds still
slept stirred started to rise and walked
among while dew soaked shoes
scattered like children's toys
gathered them into canvas bags
took home and bleached stacked
them on shelves by shape size
long femurs sideways radii end on
ribs in curving ranks like waves
fan-shaped shoulder blades
on edge like dinner plates
piles of vertebrae all
punctuated by the bovine skulls
looking out behind to the left
the right and sat back to behold
the beauty of the rhythm of the bones

———

Letter to the Artist

I received the box of little heads
you made and sent me, Winifred,
about the size of chicken eggs,
just the way I like them: Freudian,
with a clot of nascent life inside;
their faces carved with mouths and eyes,
incised with wrinkled worry lines,
and here and there a smile. Uncanny,
how you've imbued them
with personality, with life; look
so familiar I've given them
familiar names like Frank and Jim
and Cousin Mike and even that of
my ex-wife whom we'll call "her,"
to preserve domestic harmony because
even poets sometimes must explain;
I'm sure for sculptors it's the same.
Glazed, they shine and speak to me
in their different voices, on occasion
talk among themselves about me,
about which I admit I'm of two minds,
wonder if I'm being used, then realize
how foolish: does any streetwise Dante
feel he's abused by the tattooed Beatrice
that he's idolized? Not
that I'm complaining, by no means;

at the very least they amuse me,
and I confess there have been times
when they've proposed a prompt
or given me a line, sometimes a word
I didn't know I knew left me
feeling I should give them credit.
Or should I credit you?
Which of us is projecting
onto these homunculi?
Is this what's meant by "a muse"?
Who's been thinking, much less writing
these poems that I sign?

————

How To Write A Poem

for Karen who wanted to know

Your deep thoughts and/or
strong feelings do not make
a poem, any more than wanting
to cross the river makes a bridge,
nor does a metaphor like that,
nor even a well-wrought aphorism
about the anxiety of desire unless
you include the song
the wind makes the cables sing
as you're crossing and you
look down and shit yourself.
That's the real thing.

———

American Beauty

People arrived, lined up
down the street, around
the block, beleaguered,
anxious, scanning strangely
shattered faces leaving, eager
nonetheless like jumpers
on a dare. Many entering forgot
their feet and stumbled, fumbled
what they carried, mumbled
dry-mouthed words
that rose unbidden, broken
parts of speech, brief
plosive pieces, vowels
evoking unacknowledged wants.
They blinked, stared, looked
about in fear, some went
outside before, my god,
they howled, and drove away
somewhere weeping, others
went home to have
sex for consolation, but
still unable to forget, to sleep. Not
that some didn't frown,
dubious, non-plussed. Roadies
wrapped things up routinely,
took Beauty to the next town
on their chartered bus.

———

Emil's Back

Man walks into a bar.
Reggie Breaux has turned
on his stool and bent down
to pull up his recalcitrant socks,
looks up from beneath his thick
and wiry eyebrows to see who
it is. Things happen quickly now,
images begin to blur and later
no one can recall just
what happened, who did whatever
it was first. Francine Reagan, the best
nine-ball player in town looks up
before stroking the cue ball
into the unbroken pack. The bookie,
the insurance adjustor, the off-duty cop
and the undercover one, as well
as the neighborhood Don Juan
who's fucking Reggie's wife
stiffen all at once, and Bernie Boule,
the poet manqué slash bartender,
reaches instinctively for his towel just as
Sarah comes out of the Men's Room
with that look that dares you
to say something, screams
dramatically as she will do, and Emil
smiles and says, Hi, everyone! I'm back!
Therein, as always, lies a story.

———————

Coffee Break

I watch while waiting the baristas'
mating dance. Sliding behind her
as she wipes hot milk off
the steam wand, he whispers
something surely dirty in her ear.
I swear spit sprays into that coffee
when she laughs. She pats his butt
discreetly when she reaches
for a cup. My god, they're prob'ly
fucking in the break room, these two.
Remind you of us? Back in the day,
when we could not
not touch each other, when all
we had to do was say the magic word
that can be hard now to recall.
I gave him a phony name
when I ordered, just to be perverse.
Their forced bonhomie
annoys me. You want to know what
I did last weekend, make that coffee
free. They have no idea what
they're getting into, these two,
as if anyone does; how one thing
leads so strangely to what's next.
We all start out enchanted too.
He's called "Mike" four times
before I realize that's me, and I
apologize with a wink: I know
what you're up to, big guy. As I
pass her sitting by herself, she says,
You don't look like a Mike. Me:

Things aren't always what they seem.
Her eyes roll round ironically. She says,
Sit down. I'm thinking, Wha? as I take in
the tangled frizz of dirty wool
around her head, the grimy web
of creases on her cheeks, and those
entirely unexpected eyes, blue as
Antarctic ice is said to be. I haven't
been myself. Cradling with both hands
her drink, a double latte, with a little
spittle, she's kicked off her shoes,
revealing swollen feet, upturned
her purse, the better I guess
to read the future in the guts;
looks up, fixes me with those
icy blues - what must they
have seen - and sternly says, Don't
fall in love with me. Okay, I nod.
We sit in silence with our coffees, like
so many couples that you see.
The barista as he leaves, did he
just laugh and wink at me?

————————

Louise

I slept fitfully, woke dreaming,
remembering long-legged Louise
who used to wrap herself around
every part of me until I came awake
humming, mumbling Dylan's line,
Louise, and her lover, so entwined;
squeezing black tea into my cup
as the radio plays Bonnie Raitt,
They all said Louise was not half bad,
a deceiver, don't believe her.
Coincidence abounds and I'm amused.
Every little breeze seems to whisper Louise.
Until I receive an e-mail from Steve:
Louise died this morning, heart attack.

Coincidences seem not in sudden grief
portentous, but perverse, and I feel almost
threatened by their influences. Meet Suzanne
for lunch, tell her the news; she weeps.
    "But I think it's sweet," she says
through her sniffles. Life rhymes all the time,
you know, though we usually ignore it
when we're rarely even listening.
    I just bought 'The Night Watchman,'
her new book." "Whose?" "Louise Erdrich's;
it got really good reviews." She grins.
    "If the rhyme's a good one, it can make
things seem ordained; otherwise, inane,
but I think she'd be pleased with these,
    don't you, our Louise?"

———————

Only by Chance

The night air was colder and the dew
is thicker on the lawn and on the leaves
that have fallen and begun to color it.
I saw you at the bookstore yesterday.
You had just bought coffee and I started
to wave, but pulled it back when you
ducked and ran. I'm surrounded
at the gym by once pretty women
who now stagger and stare down warily,
as if looking for anything that might
trip them up. I like to think they'd smile
at me if they could, so I smile back.
When I leave the gym today, the sun
will be too hot for the sweater
that I've worn; this weather
is so changeable. It still rises
high in the sky, the sun, but
the equinox will soon take care of that.
There's one old guy who strides boyishly
around the oval track and waves
happily when he passes me
pedaling steadily away, every time
he passes me. I guess he forgets. I have
no idea who he is. Yes, I smile, but no,
I don't wave. Maybe you would
know him. I'll have to rake the leaves
this weekend. I only know you now
as you were in the past, but I'll be
at the bookstore every day next week,
browsing through Science Fiction, where
we could only meet by chance.

———

Unseen

On the coast tonight
the future has slipped ashore
in a tiny boat.

———

Swimming Pool Haiku

I peel off my suit.
You slowly as well do yours.
The smell of chlorine.

———

Heraclitus at Creekside

for Nell and Steve

You can rebuild that house
but not the river that you look across
to the mountains from it.
The house holds on to its stories
with every nail that's rusting in them.
The river rushes its own history away.
The old women in your photos
who waded girlish in that water
wave to us yesterday.

———

The Surfer

The sand that burns bare feet at noon
feels so cold at night. We shiver
on the beach and fires have been started
while we watch and wait as we have done
for all who've wrecked off this coast
over years that overlap as memories
in our minds will do. What summer was it
you and I made love at water's edge,
thinking it would be erotic to feel the tidal
in-and-out beneath us? Mostly I recall
mosquitoes, for whom the moving target
of my ass proved too great a challenge
to ignore, though we were able both
to overcome. Who was it, is of course
the question we all ask tonight as we
order pizzas, pass the joints. Someone
we'd seen walking, watching where the waves
were breaking? Was it that guy who came in
upright all the way until his board
grabbed sand and stopped abruptly,
forcing him to make that little hop?
It must have happened while we
were staring at the carelessness
before us, trying to parse the waves
and calculate how far to that horizon
as parents yelled, Come back!
That's far enough! Many say they'd spied
the ocean try to slip the unmanned surfboard
unseen back to shore. Now and then
the chopper lighting in its golden cone
the flattened waves will hover,

we'll wade farther out in hopeful dread
as jet skis skip like stones to where
under water shadows dance, take on
human shape like the rumors racing
up and down the dunes. Wanting to see
and say we've seen will hold us here
a while in lieu of the ancient need
to cover a corpse with earth lest he
forever wander between the living
and the dead. We eschew that responsibility,
bury the lost for ourselves only, worry less
about the complex enough
contingencies of fate. And yet we grieve.
There is weeping all around, some loud,
most not, for a boy who's known to none,
which for the moment must suffice.
The body will be brought in at daybreak
by waves that will tip their caps,
and bow from the waist before leaving
reverently backwards. Later we'll return
and talk about him, some will pray,
wondering still where he was from
and where he's gone and we'll be
grateful when the godly sun
has warmed again the wrinkled sand.

———————

Elegy

for Howard

A warm winter day,
the day you died.
Sitting outside barefoot,
shorts and tee shirts, drinking
coffee, teasing, scrolling
I-pad screens. Suddenly
my computer froze as someone tried to Face
Time me and I spilled my coffee when the phone
rang with the news of you and someone screamed.

Your body, crumpled,
where you'd left it, beside
your kicked-off shoes,
hinting at how quickly
you withdrew.
A good way to go? Not feeling the fear
that floods in knowing the end is near?
Or crueler on your family than
waiting bedside, suppressing
the wishing, the end foretold?
Who's to say? Besides the ones
involved and, of course,
you. We spent the rest of that
sunny Sunday stunned.

The weather turned
the day of your interment,
yet your mourners thronged.
Snow flurried, especially it seemed
to me on those of us who had
unwisely dressed for Spring.
Truth to tell, so many appeared
to effect dilution of the grieving.
Was that a good thing? Perhaps
the point? I still wished
that I could drink that liquor
straight, and simply weep alone.

Our numbers though made
a multitude of you
and the festive air
enlarged you in our hearts.
It took forever for us each
to throw our shovelful of dirt
onto your pine-boxed chest,
to register our dull thud.
Afterwards we all hugged.
Your loss made us love each other
if only for the moment. It
offered little warmth and everyone
ran quickly to their cars. I
looked around for you, but
you were gone.

Summoning your likeness,
fearing I've forgotten.
Glasses? Sometimes? Yes?
Almost but not quite
hearing your voice, a
sardonic if not obscene
riposte. We spoke of death
when last we spoke. Ironic,
or not? You'd just bought
a family plot. Premonition?
You shrugged and grinned. We joked.
We swore to send a sign. I'll Face
Time you, you said. We
were interrupted then, as we've
been finally once again.

Fat, black flies,
bumble bees.
Spring now truly here,
though last night a freeze.
The seasons always wrestle this way
as they're changing, don't they?
Do you see that from your now
more comprehensive view? Do
the soul and body wrestle too?

It's no longer about you, you know.
You've gone on and left a hole
where there used to be my friend.
More often now you'll be
one of those framed photos
on the shelf. You've crossed
an imagined line, you've gone
from here to where.
The deaths that move us
most leave us asking
the questions we can't answer,
that drive us to religion or,
in emergency, to art.
This pain too will go away
but like the rain that's due
tomorrow, another like it
will occur. Perhaps the best
thing we can do is keep
a weather eye on our hearts.

———————

Grief

It's the growing thing,
roots in any soil,
flowers in any weather,

It burns less when wet;
tears work well for that.
Salt will leach the rancor out.

It will grow long limbs,
leaved with memories.
You can rest within their shade.

———

This Old Couch

I'm sitting on the couch on the back of which
and to each side of me Charlie and Rosie
are standing, from where with a glance
at each other they fall on the cushions
and collapse screaming into me.
Then each to the other side
and making sure midway to tussle
they crawl across my lap, reach up
and climb past my shoulders til again
they are standing on the back
of this old couch. They do this tirelessly
over and over until they don't. Is this
the stuff of poetry? Very soon
they will outgrow it, never again
be so unselfconscious, so nakedly playful
with me or with each other, but for now
are still in Eden and have brought me
however briefly to be back there with them.

———

Ruby Rolled Her Eyes

The time that your small daughter
set her bag of doll's clothes on the floor
and I feigned I couldn't pick it up,
I grunted, I groaned, I strained,
and finally I complained, I can't,
and Ruby rolled her eyes.
She lifted it with ease.
Her innocent eyes said gently, See?
I seemed to be amazed. How
did you do that? I exclaimed.
She shrugged, and I tried again,
with an even greater show of failure,
thinking this would please her in the end.
She frowned and cut her eyes,
stared hard at the bag
and raised it with one little hand
looking at me with precocious
yet sympathetic disbelief.
You said she talked of it for weeks,
you'd seen her rehearse alone
the story in her room.
I'd love to know
how she changed it over time.
I'm listening to Thelonious Monk
play "Ruby My Dear,"
which reminds me
always of her, and of you,
to whom I write this morning wondering
what to have for breakfast –
What would you? –
with the cream cheese on these bagels,
with the dreadful news on mute,
while thinking also of searching yesterday
through the Lost Locks box at the gym,

and having just been perusing the Tao Te Ching
in the bathroom, where I'm best able
to be in the moment,
despite always multi-tasking.
The news is not good.
It rarely is of late. Perhaps its
oxymoronic sameness reassures.
While I was toweling dry the other day,
the guy who seems always not to want
to put his goddam pants on was on
a rant about the war and I walked out
in disgust, leaving my lock hanging
limply from the latch,
to find myself thinking yesterday
how they all look the same,
those shackle-shapes.
The awkward, shifting heaviness
of the damp and flimsy cardboard box
had me suddenly nonplussed,
and I stood there hefting it,
trying to account for the weight
of my feelings. The first time
I lifted a corpse, I'd thought,
having given up its soul it would be lighter.
The head and limbs lolled loosely
like a puppet's, joined together but
with string. The eyes were dull
as rocks. There were so many.
The hell with it, I said.
What can you do? You
make your choice and wait; what
comes around they call your fate.
Yet I regret. As is my wont.
Words aren't more true because they rhyme,
any more than a clock contains the time,
but there are real things

for which we've yet no name,
and the body's gyve will gall the soul, so
even a facetious word may balm.
Is the task really as the Tao says
to accept? Let's imagine
your daughter and I one day will meet,
in passing, at some airport, say,
where flakes of paint and plaster spiral
from the ceiling. The cafeteria's deserted,
food-encrusted plates still on the counter, seats
are over-turned, glass crunches under feet, valises
wait forlornly on the luggage carousel. I'll try
to help her with her bag, but she'll protest:
It's not heavy. I'll insist,
and then I'll feign I can't.
I'll grunt, and groan and strain,
and when she lifts it up with ease I'll look
for some faint sign that she recalls,
like a tensing of those small muscles
around her eloquent eyes.
Is it not in such a stirring of memory,
in a reach for words amidst the wreckage,
that our hope, at least in part, must lie?
Ruby of song "would rather die
than say goodbye," but there will
sooner than later come a day
when we must each do both.
Write, please, tell me you're okay.

————————

The Playhouse

Rosie's red playhouse.
Looking out through its windows
she creates the world.

———

Up and Down the Dune

My grandson at two and a half
chasing a beach ball over the dune
cried, Nee hep! as he started to fall
and I took his tiny hand.
When I slipped on the climb back up
he turned and asked, Nee hep?
extending his arm to me,
as the sand began to flow faster
through the neck of the hourglass.

———

Primary Reader

for Zerna Sharp

I was always ambivalent
about Dick and Jane,
but not their dog, Spot,
who chiefly served to run when they said,
"Run, Spot. Run,"
and for them to see when one
said to the other,
"Look. See Spot run,"
and for me as well as you, no doubt,
if you are of a certain age,
to learn to read about.
That poor dog
had to run a lot when life and language
seem from here to have been
if not simple, simpler
than now when words may often be
– Good grief, Charlie Brown –
polysyllabic,
and one thought can forever
after another run,
having crossed its path.
Spot sniffed one day some pheromone,
slipped his leash, was later found
sleeping at a stranger's door,
was taken in and belly-scratched
as if he had never been before.

This is as good, I guess, as any time
to confess that I used to
- dare I say it? -
read ahead, to see what happened next,
the unforeseen result of which
was boredom, re-reading it all
again and again and again
at Dick and Jane's expense
– would they never change? –
until one day Spot returned,
wagging excitedly his tail and drooling
everywhere, clutching softly but firmly
in his mouth a warm and wiggling,
freshly captured meaning.

———————

Nothing Special

We were all dejectedly hunched in front
of the TV screen watching again and again
our downtown neighbors scream and scramble
like roaches when a light's turned on, as
five year-old Susie walked through talking
into a cordless telephone that we'd never
bothered to remove from its unconnected
fixture on the wall, an *objet d'art*
whose ringing now would make us all
stop, look up in alarm, as Susie did
when she said to her imaginary friend,
Delphine, "The president is a scumbag",
and we leapt so suddenly
in parental horror to remonstrate
that we terrified her for repeating a word
she'd likely just then overheard, now
made unforgettable and lent a valence
that would make it a weapon in her not
far off resentful adolescence. Helpless
otherwise to calm her, we said, "Here.
Delphine wants to talk to you," but she
pushed the phone away and said, "I hate
Delphine. I want ice cream," a winning
tactic at the moment. Meanwhile, Wolf Blitzer
said they'd found the shooter's car, trunk full
of automatic weapons. Nothing special there.
Susie ate her ice cream silently and
with glistening eyes, just stared.

———————

Politics and Romance

I see Mandelstam and Akhmatova
arching their Slavic eyebrows in
their graves this winter, knowing better
than we the changes coming with this weather.
The ground hardens making footsteps
sound more loudly in the night time,
people turn their collars up
for warmth which makes their faces
harder to see, fingers
are too stiff for writing letters. Can you
understand these signs I'm making? Please
tell no one that you knew me
once, when we were young.

———

Arlington National Cemetery

Hiding in the leaves,
we watched men being buried,
boys toying with grief.

______

Fall Anxiety

Steamy autumn night.
Trees clutch tight their dry brown leaves,
worried something's wrong.

______

All Things in Their Turn

The farts of ancient aurochs buried deep
in arctic ice are rising up to taunt us
for our well-intentioned if not willful
ignorance of which we're all at fault
     denying burning up our home to heat
     our houses cool our cars and cube our water
     even launch us to another planet once
     we're done with this one breathing
     ancient air more every day as geologic
     cladding steams away
          like morning mist used to at the now
          dry man-made lake upstate where we
          chained our rowboat yearly to a tree
          before we left and now it dangles
          ten feet up a neo-plastic bag
          caught in the branches
               soon to be a nest for the terrifying
               scion of some pterosaur hoping
               we'll return and make him lunch
               if he can stomach us thus all things
               in their turn eat or/and are eaten

because we can't believe the earth
will ever die any more than we despite
the evidence of the graves in every
town the coffins that will compact
over eons underground even with
the superfluity of concrete shells
      meant to keep I guess our molecules
      intact or something in ourselves interred
      some sulphurous bat-winged devil
      out of hell that's scratching at
      the inside of its egg
driven by the fear of what we don't know to cling
to what we do for good or ill so that it makes
less sense the more we think it through
as if the birds the plants the planet
we ourselves or what may be within us
were not all the same and whatever
anybody any longer means
by god.

———————

Bufo

Bufo Speaks Up

Clinging to the un-
derside of my green patio um-
brella, does the toad know
he's up-
side down, or does he think
it's I
who is li-
able to fall,
or rise?
He slits his eyes
at me and says,
What's up?
What a wise
guy.

Then Does Stand-Up

You think this is funny?
This ain't funny.
Before you know it
you'll be in Chattanooga
clinging sideways to a sail
in a salt-water storm
while a giant green
post-anthropocene amphibian
with a prehensile steel tongue
for catching flies the size of Cessnas
looks at you like lunch.
What'll you say then,
big boy?
Now that's funny.
Doncha think?
Or doncha?

———

61

Botany Quiz

Without leaves the trees
cannot wave only tremble
their bony fingers groping hungrily
for air they cannot breathe.
When Spring arrives and leaves them
breezes fill their greening sails
and the soil in which they're seeded
seems a sea of dreams
on which they float. And when
we leave will we come bodiless alive
underground, in the air, somewhere
we don't believe in or are we
the very thing?

Chief Complaint

Weak and fever-ridden if not wracked
with pain as God's white-coated avatars
hand-comb nervously their hair and try
to make some sense of signs and symptoms
and the arcane blood tests that belie them
with improbable false positives and their
negative counterparts saying "something
is not right here" to themselves "let's
just wait and see" to me while I watch
deliriously on the flat wall-mounted
tee vee screen a hurricane of heretofore
unrecorded size strength and severity
take aim directly per the European
model at my home a scene I've sometimes
dreamed but haven't seen before the time-
worn script transfixing us with such a
dreadful swelling thrill I almost hope it
hits so we can sigh with post-calamity
relief and ask each other "how was that
for you" when out of the whispering
hallway appears an elderly little brown-
skinned woman unsure even if it's okay
to smile who strangely albeit kindly asks
in her second-language syntax "what sir
for drink will you be liking when you
today lunch had" stopping me dead
in my tracks and pulling me in a
straight line from the time and place

to which I've desperately been clinging
flinging me through the spinning viral
wall into tranquility so utter I can not
speak nor hear the voices in alarm calling
my name see their fearful faces feel
the needles puncturing my veins until
she appears shouting on TV from
the coast into shrieking wind and rain
the storm south finally is turning my
house to spare and elsewhere its
wrath unleashing relief and I admit a little
schadenfreude with me leaving saying
"You were soon better feeling" bowing
as she backwards from the room goes,
I sometimes wistfully what happened
where I went wonder try in vain
about it to explain and myself find
awkwardly if not ungrammatically
asking "up with that, what is?"

———————

Resuscitation

It's getting to be old hat, the number of times I've died
and been brought back. When I do take my last gasp
 I hope to go like Zack who collapsed on the treadmill
 that spat him out like a seed from between its teeth,
 so that I can't help but smile to remember.
 I thought he was joking for the eternal nanosecond
before I was shoved aside by the excited
 cpr-trained guys because that's the sort of thing
 Zack was known to do, then jump up:
the joke's on you. What was it like? you ask.
I can tell you this: it's life that is the dreaming thing
that you will almost, not quite remember
when you wake, linger, drag your heavy feet across
 the line and try recalling who it was and where and why,
leaving you a sweet affection for it all, hang back a while
as anxious strangers call your name. I saw God, of course;
he looked like my friend, John, who insists
that he does not exist. Nothing bores, I know,
like someone else's dreams and remember more
 is something I can't do. Yet I appreciate the practice;
it ameliorates the fear of falling. The going's not
the problem; it's the coming back that's fraught for me
with rueful feelings though, I hope, likely not for you.
I still imagine Zack to sit straight up or more
 discreetly wink at me from his box and say,
"I'm almost done here, you can have it next."

———————

Vernal Equinox

It's the first day of Spring! she says.
Good to know. I almost never do
know what day it is. Breakfast helps,
pharmaceuticals *au jus*: coffee
and ten pills, various colors, shapes and sizes
from one of seven little boxes,
orient me, minimally; still,
there's room for error any time
I have to choose, given little evidence
what week or month or heaven help me
year it is, so yes, an imperfect tool,
no less than the language that I use,
but I work with what I've got,
try to remember which one
keeps my lipids low, which my pressure,
my digestion, urine flow and equanimity
within parameters that permit me
to go on, such that any variance
in behavior, up or down - too sleepy
or too gaseous or growly -
elicits this fail-safe:
"Did you take your pills this morning?"

Curious how people say,
"There's something in the air,"
so blithely that it's rare we ask,
"What?" I can almost feel the ions.
Whatever the date is the light will last
as long today as the night and I am
energized. Woke up at four
to the shifting of the seasons,
went down to find the dog
barking blindly at the glass
and let him out and out
he ran and ran around in circles
like dogs will do. Long ago
people less well-clothed than we
erected massive stones in circles
to more exactly date and celebrate –
so we suppose, knowing no more
of their thinking than they did
of the Poles – the lengthening of the light,
and we've been putting names and numbers
to our days since then if not before,
and just no doubt as it did them
it proffers us at least
an illusion of control
over the time of our lives,
when and where otherwise
we'd have only the fail-safe of –
and it is by no means nothing –
the here and now.

———

Spring Haiku

Fireside sex in Spring.
Water whistles in the wood.
Rivers melt upstream.

———

Summer Haiku

Bare skin on the beach.
The roar, then the ebbing tide.
There's sand in your kiss.

———

Letter to Jack, in Paris

So you're in Paris,
and as your postcard implies,
I'm not. Isn't that the message
of those three-by-fives we used to
and some still do flaunt
with foreign stamps? I said before
you left, did I not, that you'd
regret not going to our fiftieth,
even if you traded for your first
with Jill? You could have wed them,
so to speak. You needn't be
embarrassed. A lot of guys would
envy you. I'm pretty sure
that I do. Can I say that? There
were fewer of us this year, Jack,
for the obvious reason. I used to
think it was only the more
accomplished guys who went,
to get themselves patted on
the back; you know what I
mean? Was that just my resentment,
a lack of self-esteem, or mere
indifference? When I get out
of jail, I don't tell the driver,
floor it, man, I'm late
for my high school reunion.
And why didn't you ever go?

Doesn't matter. This one was
different, this was arms around
the shoulders, Jack, this was, Glad
you're still alive. When I was driving
home, against my own better
judgment and the law, the oncoming
lights began to sparkle and I
realized I was crying. What is it about
remembering that we like
just for itself? I too was once in
Paris, and you weren't, my friend,
and I was only twenty, and
I wouldn't trade the memory
of it for another visit. Do me
a favor. Have a photo taken
of the two of you,
beneath the Arc de T.,
on a picture postcard
perfect day.

————————

The Knot

It was my own name thrown
in the timbre of her voice
that turned me back,
transfixed us both before
her friend who sat astonished
as if two cars had crashed
beside their sidewalk table,
spilled her glass. We sort of
hugged, in a flustering mix
of anxieties and affections,
quickly parted to an arm's length
to look for the old face
in the new and clutching each
our own urbanity said, "Wow,
It's really you! How are you?"
and watched entranced
a movie unreel of the lives
we'd once and the ones we
afterwards could have led,
measured against the timelines
of the more unlikely ones
we had. "Married? Kids?
Me too." Given a chance
once more to entwine those
threads however casually we
said only, "So. Good to see you.
All the best." And parted,
fingering the small knot left
in the otherwise unsurprising
unwinding of our day.

———

Left Behind

Does love never visit
without its *vade mecum*,
heartbreak,
in a little leather satchel,
set down often by the door,
seems only accidentally
left behind,
and when you shout,
Hey! You forgot something!
a hand waves high in the air
with no look back, and
Keep it!
hollered over the shoulder?
One must admit, however,
sometimes the leather is exquisite.

————————

Embarkation

Which more pain entails:
the disappearance of land
or that of the sails?

———

Arrivals

They come through yawning,
red-eyed arrivals,
pulling their lives behind them.

———

The Hole in Us

Beneath the engines' storied roaring,
there's a subtler sound above,
of a hole being torn in the sky by a jet
just now leaving town. We persist
in thinking of air as emptiness,
an almost imaginary thing we suck
involuntarily into ourselves until
we don't, without which we are nothing
or something altogether other. Even less
substantial: gravity, electricity, radio
waves, these thoughts. We know
these things exist because we sense
and measure their effects, just as
when a loved one leaves it leaves
a hole in us that no one sees but
you could fly a jet airliner through.

———

A Differential Calculus of My Feelings

Listening in the ambulance to the insistent siren,
trying like the rabbit dying in an eagle's claws
just to enjoy the ride, amusing myself guessing
from my compromised position where the hell
we are by all that's flashing past. The roof
of our house needs replacing, traffic's backed up
as usual on the bypass, there's your office
building, where's your car? Clouds are massing
gray beyond the mountains west. You've been
hurting more than you've been saying,
I can tell, afraid to scare me by complaining,
just as I am you. More often lately when
you think, I answer; when I sigh, you wake.
I'd thought once at our age we'd have seen
the best of what was promised, never guessed
how much distance we could cover simply
by moving closer to each other. Sometimes,
says the eagle, I'm surprised myself.

———————

Venus in Venice

Would you please tilt the blinds,
she asked, the sun is in my eyes.
Half-dreaming too, I teased myself and her
with the wand, working it back and forth,
causing the Adriatic light to strobe
to which she in her sleepy way responded:
Hey! Stop that!
What puppeteer invented
this hidden mechanism with its
curious tiny wheels and locks
for the slats to climb up and down
in place like our hearts
every time we pull the cord?
There is romance in this ingenuity
I thought as I curled up hard
against her back and said,
Those Venetians!
to which she responded,
It was Persians, and don't
even think of having sex.

———

Atlantic Sunrise

Low tide, early morning.
The beach in its underwear still,
too tired to hide the evidence
of the night's debauchery.
Soon it will rise and wash itself,
sweep the empty shells
and carcasses, smooth
the wrinkled carpet, open
windows to the sky before
the children come relentless
with expectation that things
will always be the way
they were yesterday.

———

What It's Like to Be A Dolphin
for Abby and Sam

Four dolphins surfing
always astonishes those
who are not dolphins

———

Ocean Grammar

Dolphins have their say.
Their thin black fins like commas
punctuate the waves.

———

Charlie Chaplin on the Coast

Watching the stints play their hunt and peck
part in this timeless tidal drama, chasing
the ebbing surf to poke their beaks
into bubbles in the mud and then - eek - dancing
back at the last possible chance in their
comically pawky way, that awkward
stiff-legged gait, holding onto their hats,
twirling their canes, kicking their heels, risking
it all with insouciant aplomb, I recall
how it feels to wait for a cue, hoping
this time I won't drop a line or do something
 wrong so you scrimp on applause.
But what does it mean, to do it again,
and again and again and again and
never change the routine? What's to be gained
but the script maintained? Wouldn't you like
a spell of trying a new way, running, say,
headlong into the water, come what may?

———————

The Actor Takes the "D" Train

It's a small world and it gets crowded,
with everyone I've ever known
or heard of showing up, as if
at a traveling cocktail party.
Have you seen Bill? asks a woman
I recognize but never met,
turning from the map with mischief
in her eyes. *Not for years,* I say.
Then Bill of course appears,
as always right on cue.
Hiding behind the arras again, old boy?
To be or not to be, he says,
rolling ruefully his eyes.
He'd been rehearsing lines, mirrored
in a darkened window of the film-strip.
Bien fait, I say, as he grabs a strap
and keeps his feet when we turn
sharply, metal screaming in the dark.
"Next stop, Fordham Road!"
a voice above or in my head intones.
Please, that tired old college dream?
Or a movie, winks Fellini, kissing
Anita Ekberg sloppily on the cheek.
Caro, stop, everyone is looking.
Note to self, I think: Call Debbie
about audition, that part
was made for me. It is me! I could play it
in my sleep. *That's the problem,*

I can hear her now. *You need to bring it*
every night. Oh Deb, I moue, *I would*
for you. Imagine that. I do. And there I go,
just as we get to my stop and I
have to stand up, tumescent once again.
"Doors opening. Watch your step!"
Exeunt, all shoulders and elbows.
I have always depended
on the kindness of strangers.
Does everyone do this? I live mostly
in my head, not that it's a secret though
it does seem secretive, and there you are,
waiting patiently if unsure to meet me
here at the end of the line.

———————

The Audition

The seasons compete for the starring role
In the planet's new weather production.
One day the world's encased in ice,
tulips rise next day out of the mulch,
dooming themselves so early,
making the old man nervous
for himself as well. Variation
can be nice but these stark untimely
contrasts are a bitch. At seventy years
and degrees he hates wool socks,
they make him itch. Should he walk
in sandals every day, wear salmon-
colored shorts though it might snow,
look like some hot-house flower,
move to Hawaii in his mind?
One coast is perennially on fire,
the other another inch monthly
under sea, and everything in between
is blown away or sucked
into the ground. Should he take a lesson
from that dog who's sniffing out
a propitious place to shit, who
as he sleeps, snorts, twitches, dreams
he's chasing rabbits, and paws fecklessly
the insubstantial surface of the earth?
Should he take advantage of the age
to audition for a role requiring
liver spots before the blinding
lime-lit edge of time? Better he thinks
a late bloomer than a frozen tulip be,
but then again who knows?
One lives if ever only rarely
long enough to see.

What's New

It seems to me at my worst moments,
when the best that I can do
is stay upright, the world itself
is coming to an end; disaster looms
at every turn. Is it but a truism
that old men see ruin all about,
project their own demise
daily more onto the news: politics,
the weather, music, sports, all going
rotten at the core, while youngsters
teach us patiently how to use
the latest geospatial app, lead us
gently by the hand, say reassuringly,
*Like this. That's right, see? There's
where your grave will be.* Good to know,
I guess, that plans are underway,
our needs are being addressed, but really,
they should worry more
about themselves, the mess
we're leaving them. My father
on his deathbed, and I'm already past
that age, seemed to struggle at the end,
not from heroics, but as if held back,
by some shirt tail-tugging regret,
until we told him, *We're okay.
You can go.* At which point
he deeply sighed, closed his eyes and died.

I found a photograph the other day
of him, still a boy but close enough
to manhood to see it looming,
a large cloth bag hanging by a strap
from his shoulder to his knees
as he smiled at me from a corner
on a chilly Spring, Maine day,
confident as only sixteen years can be,
that the newspapers he's peddling,
despite their raucous headlines
and their obits, report nothing
he can't handle. And
for a long time to his yet likely
slowly growing dismay,
they don't.

———

Hambone

for Kathy

She had often talked about the coffins
leaning empty up against the houses,
later full and stacked high in the streets,
something else to squat behind
when they played hide-and-seek,
during the Nineteen-eighteen
influenza epidemic, details
she could not have known
having just been born, I later realized,
in August of that year, and so those coffins
and those games must have been for her
remembered first by someone else.

On her deathbed she sat abruptly up
and talked urgently albeit not
intelligibly for an hour or more
to my sister, as if she'd been waiting
all day for her, then lay back
smiling, satisfied, and died.
The lights in the next room flashed
on and off, every now and then
for a few days, never again,
according to everyone
who says that they were there,
amid our noisy weeping.

The devil's beating his wife
with a hambone, my mother said,
one day when I was small and we
heard thunder in a clear blue sky.
My questions were: why
was he beating her, why
a hambone, and why,
when there was thunder
in a clear blue sky?
She looked at me and smiled,
It's a way to talk about
something we don't understand.

———

These Things

These things that will not happen long ago
did or did not cause all those things
that happened tomorrow. You see
how hard it is to pin things down?
They slip forth and back in time, elide
their beginnings and their ends. To make it
more personal: will I remember you
yesterday? Did I forget you tomorrow?
This is not a game though it is a poem;
makes its own rules, like speech does,
much the same, but so do you and I,
trying to write the story of our lives,
our loves, our alibis and wonder
where to begin, how far back
we have to go, don't know
where and when it had to end,
so best to start here, now,
in this house, in this chair,
writing to you, drinking
this beer, thinking
these things will happen
long ago again.

———

Back To Where It Began

Raise your hand
if you would go back
to where it began, find yourself
there now, let this be your map.
Orient yourself, though I hear true North
is moving once again. Memories,
like pictures of your parents taken
just before it all went bad, when most things
had no name and people had to point,
will gratify but still may make you sad.
It all looks smaller, doesn't it? Nothing's
changed of course is why you left:
you wanted more. Still do, though you know now
so much of what's involved and suspect
worse is yet to come. There's your folks'
first house, the muddled nest of shrubs
and branches you all huddled in between
the open fields and legendary woods,
with a screen door that wouldn't fully shut
but slapped a rhythm maddeningly irregular
in the slightest wind, one day trapped
a garden snake half-inside,
half-out and everybody screamed,
no one more alarmed no doubt
than the hapless herpetological
symbol of evil itself. Inset: the mythical tree,
on which no apple ever grew but
of whose leaves that curious shade
of green has long inspired a yearning
you cannot satisfactorily explain. The old
neighborhood, where you roamed wild,
taunted baboons and bonobos for losing
evolution's last audition in your
rebellious teen-age years, when you

shaved a hairless streak down
the center of your back and ran away
with friends with whom you rehearsed
hand signs for what you could not
otherwise express, imagined how
your parents would be shocked. Far off
downwind you see him, recognize him
by his bearing even from behind among
the furrier ones otherwise just like him, and
he senses, most likely smells you, separates
himself and squints, strides your way
and stops, bends down and draws
a line in the dirt, and looks expectantly at you,
who bemused by if nothing else his nakedness
opt to play along, and draw another line
that bends back to where it began.
You look at your own younger self as he gapes,
astonished with recognition, and
you put each the palm of a hand on a pane
of the unseen glass between you,
knowing everything that ever was still is,
as I hold up my hand now to yours.

———

The Lighthouse Keeper's Window

The pictured frame of the window through
which the photo of the lighthouse was taken
is a wave from the artist to you.

—

Beau's Tanka

Starless sky tonight.
We're sailing blindly in space.
My black dog's unseen,
jumps up abruptly and barks,
snorts, and then lies down again.

———

Acknowledgments

Thanks to the folks at Amplify for steering me through the shoals of their world, and especially to Lauren Magnussen for her enthusiastic support.

I owe more than they likely appreciate to the many people who have read these poems as they originally appeared in recent years, to the friends who casually proffered encouragement, and to Jim Finn, Brendan Reilly, and Brian Gallagher who each offered it at a moment when, unknown to them, it was particularly meaningful and gratifying. Finally, thanks to John McEveety Woodruff for his friendship and always astute criticism that made almost every poem better than it would otherwise have been.

And of course, that I owe everything to Christie Aderholt and our family goes without saying, but I say it again here anyway.

About the Author

Ron Berube was born in Maine and raised on a series of military bases, and educated at Fordham University and the University of Virginia, but first and most formatively at Gonzaga College High School in Washington, DC. He has worked as a New York City cab driver, a metal foundry laborer, an insurance adjuster, and for thirty-five years as a Psychiatric Nurse. He published three short stories in the late 1970s, and has been writing poetry seriously since he retired about seven years ago. *The Tearing Sound* is his first collection. He lives in Virginia with his wife, and gratefully near their children and grandchildren.